Learn About Urban Life

Life in a Suburban City

Lizann Flatt

Crabtree Publishing Company

www.crabtreebooks.com

Author: Lizann Flatt
Editor-in-Chief: Lionel Bender
Editors: Simon Adams and Molly Aloian
Proofreader: Adrianna Morganelli
Project coordinator: Kathy Middleton
Photo research: Ben White
Designer and makeup: Ben White
Production coordinator: Amy Salter
Production: Kim Richardson
Prepress technician: Amy Salter
Consultant: Amy Caldera, M.Sc., Elementary School
Publishing Consultant, Writer, and Former Teacher

Main cover photo: Downtown Los Angeles, California,
sprawls out behind Beverly Hills.
Inset cover photo: Family barbecues are a favorite
pastime in the suburbs.

This book was produced for Crabtree Publishing
Company by Bender Richardson White

Photographs and reproductions:
© Alamy: cover inset (Radius Images)
© BigStockPhoto: cover main image (David McShane)
© Getty Images: pages 1 and 16 (Asger Carlsen),
    6 (Marc Volk), 7 (ImageBank), 18 (Wire Image),
    23 (AFP), 26, 27 (Wire Image)
© iStockphoto.com: page 10 (Jim Kruger)
© Topfoto: pages 14 (Ullsteinbild), 29 (Caro/Kaiser)
© Sara Jayne Boyers: page 17
© www.shutterstock.com: Headline image (Gerry
    Boughan), pages 4 (Alphonse Tran), 5 (Fotolistic),
    8 (Rodolfo Arpia), 9 (Sergei Butorin), 11 (Sam D.
    Cruz), 12 (CJP Designs), 13 and 15 (Xavier
    Marchani), 19 (Mike Liu), 20 (John Blanton),
    21 (iofoto), 22 (Jose Gil), 24 (Gerry Boughan),
    25 (Jose Gil), 28 (Thorsten)

Acknowledgments:
The author wishes to thank Sara Jayne Boyers, resident
of Los Angeles, for verifying the information about
L.A. and Papik family for the photograph on page 17.

Library and Archives Canada Cataloguing in Publication

Flatt, Lizann
    Life in a suburban city / Lizann Flatt.

(Learn about urban life)
Includes index.
ISBN 978-0-7787-7394-8 (bound).--ISBN 978-0-7787-7404-4 (pbk.)

    1. City and town life--Juvenile literature. 2. Suburban life--
Juvenile literature. 3. Los Angeles Suburban Area (Calif.)--
Juvenile literature. I. Title. II. Series: Learn about urban life

HT351.F53 2010   j307.74   C2009-906249-6

Library of Congress Cataloging-in-Publication Data

Flatt, Lizann.
    Life in a suburban city / Lizann Flatt.
        p. cm. -- (Learn about urban life)
    Includes index.
    ISBN 978-0-7787-7404-4 (pbk. : alk. paper) --
ISBN 978-0-7787-7394-8 (reinforced library binding : alk. paper)
    1. City and town life--Juvenile literature. 2. City and town life--
California--Los Angeles--Juvenile literature. 3. Suburban life--
Juvenile literature. 4. Los Angeles Suburban Area (Calif.)--
Juvenile literature. I. Title. II. Series.

    HT152.F577 2010
    307.76--dc22

                                        2009042424

Crabtree Publishing Company
www.crabtreebooks.com   1-800-387-7650

Printed in the USA/122009/BG20091103

Published in Canada
Crabtree Publishing
616 Welland Ave.
St. Catharines, Ontario
L2M 5V6

Published in the United States
Crabtree Publishing
PMB 59051
350 Fifth Avenue, 59th Floor
New York, New York 10118

Published in the United Kingdom
Crabtree Publishing
Maritime House
Basin Road North, Hove
BN41 1WR

Published in Australia
Crabtree Publishing
386 Mt. Alexander Rd.
Ascot Vale (Melbourne)
VIC 3032

Contents

Urban Areas

Cities and towns where thousands or millions of people live and work close together are called **urban areas**. They are usually filled with many buildings, roads, and traffic. Places with far fewer people, such as villages, are called **rural areas**. They have fewer buildings and roads, and are quieter places.

▼ Here, in the center of the city of Montreal, Canada, most buildings are tall. They provide a lot of space for people to live and work yet take up only a small area on the ground.

Within a city, there are many **neighborhoods**. A neighborhood is an area where many people live, shop, and relax together. Most cities have a central "downtown" area, with many offices and stores, and living areas near the edge of the city. These outer areas are known as **suburbs**. This book looks at life in the suburbs of cities such as Los Angeles in the United States.

No matter where people live, they need food, clean fresh water, and shelter. They also need **energy** such as electricity to heat and light their homes and to cook their food. These essential items are called **resources**.

In a city, large amounts of resources have to be delivered to many people every day. To do this, the city needs a lot of workers and quick and easy ways to reach everyone living there.

People need homes. In the city of Hong Kong, China, many familes live together in tall buildings. Each family lives in a space called an apartment.

At city markets like this one in Myanmar, Burma, residents can buy food that is grown on nearby farms.

Cities are often near a sea coast, or beside a large river or lake. There, the **residents**—the people who live in the city—use the water for drinking, cleaning, and as a **transportation** route. Other natural resources such as oil or food from farms are brought to the city from the surrounding countryside. **Factories**, offices, and stores in the city provide jobs for lots of workers.

"Services" is the name for all the needs a city must provide for the people that live there. The housing service makes sure everyone has a home. The transportation service provides buses and trains to move people around the city quickly. Other services provide street cleaning and lighting, and deliver clean water to every building. The wastewater system takes away **sewage** and rainwater.

▼ People from all sorts of different backgrounds and cultures live in most cities today.

Big cities face problems with having a lot of people. Roads can become so crowded with cars and trucks that traffic jams happen. Pollution or smog from **exhaust** from cars, factories, and buildings makes the air unhealthy to breathe. Cities have to collect tons of trash. They can run out of land to build houses on or places to put garbage.

Some cities also have problems providing extra services for new people wanting to live there. The **immigrants** may come from rural areas or from overseas.

Factories produce waste gases that can pollute the air. Chemicals in polluted air can damage the concrete, wood, and steel of buildings, kill trees, and poison lakes.

Districts and Zones

Cities often make **laws** that say how large its buildings can be. They also make laws to control what types of buildings and activities can happen in different areas. These areas are called districts or zones. Factories operate in **industrial** zones. **Commercial** zones are where businesses and offices carry on their activities. People live in **residential** zones.

▼ This photo taken from the air shows the residential area of a city. Each house looks similiar and each takes up the same amount of space.

Cities make parks, like this one in Sydney, Australia, to provide areas for people to enjoy. They often include trees, grass, benches, playgrounds, and walking areas.

Zone rules make sure homes are not built near the worst noise and pollution from factories or the busy traffic from commercial areas. In residential zones, areas can be set aside for parks. Residential areas that are outside busy downtown locations and close to the edge of the city are known as suburbs.

Welcome to L.A.

Los Angeles, or L.A., is the city with the second largest **population**—the number of residents—in the United States. The four million residents are called Angelenos. Many have an hispanic or Latino, African, Middle Eastern, Asian, Native American, or European background. Los Angeles is made up of many suburbs—areas away from the city center, each with its own stores, schools, and houses.

A TV crew filming in the L.A. surburb of Venice Beach. Hollywood, the home of movie making, is another suburb of L.A.

A map of North America showing the city of Los Angeles on the west coast of the United States. It lies within the state of California.

The city covers an area of about 470 square miles (1,222 sq km). Downtown Los Angeles features skyscrapers and commercial offices, City Hall and **government** buildings, and theaters. The city is busy during the day but few people live in the downtown area. Most people live one suburb and journey to and from work in another suburb each day.

Los Angeles is known for the freeways that weave in, out, and around the city connecting all of its many suburbs.

Spreading Out

One of the first peoples to live in the area of L.A. were Tongva Indians. They lived there many hundreds of years ago. In the 1780s, Spanish people set up a town in the area. In the late 1800s, a railroad was built linking L.A. with the rest of America. By the early 1900s, Los Angeles had grown to be a city with a seaport and a freshwater supply. People came to live in the warm climate.

▼ In 1901, Figueroa Street looked much different than it does today. The street was small, with a few big houses. Today, it is one of the longest, busiest streets in L.A.

Los Angeles is made of many suburbs. Most of them are filled with low-rise houses, schools, and other buildings.

With a lot of flat land around to build on, Los Angeles spread out quickly. Today, the city is a collection of many districts, neighborhoods, and suburbs. No one area is set aside for industrial buildings, but factories are generally built near railroad lines or freeways. Today, the downtown area is also a center of world trade and **commerce**.

Daily Life

In the suburbs of L.A, most families have their own houses. Some families live in apartment buildings. Almost all of the people with jobs leave their homes and travel some distance to work each day. Most of them travel to work by car. Because the suburbs usually have only one freeway in and out, these major roadways can be busy for much of the day.

▼ In suburban neighborhoods, a single family lives in a home with its own front and back yards.

16

Most families shop for food, clothing, and other items at suburban shopping plazas. Others shop in downtown streets famous for their stores, or in one of the city's many commercial areas.

The weather in L.A. is usually warm so Angelenos like to be outside enjoying themselves. The city is located near the mountains and Pacific Ocean, so even in winter you can see cars on the roads with snowskis or surfboards tied to racks.

School, Rest, and Play

Los Angeles has hundreds of public schools plus many **charter schools** and **private schools**. Most schools start in early September and run to mid-June when the summer holidays start. Some schools have so many students enrolled that they stay open all year long. At these schools, groups of students attend at different times of the year with their holidays spread throughout.

▼ Almost 4,000 students attend Manual Arts High School in L.A. Here, the Jazz Combo performs at the Los Angeles Film Festival.

The city runs many neighborhood parks for people to enjoy. Some parks are specially for dogs, and others are for skateboarders. There are public libraries, golf courses, children's play areas, ball fields, soccer fields, tennis courts, swimming pools, and hiking trails. There are many public beaches, museums, and the Los Angeles Zoo.

▼ Basketball is such a popular sport in Los Angeles it has two different NBA teams: the Los Angeles Lakers and the Los Angeles Clippers.

Transportation

Most people in Los Angeles travel by car on the many freeways, highways, and wide urban streets. Others use **public transportation**. Local buses travel to nearby shopping areas and hospitals.

Traveling to and from work is known as commuting. Commuter bus services connect the suburbs with downtown during morning and evening rush hours.

A commuter railroad service moves people across southern California, connecting Los Angeles with other urban areas.

20

To help commuters get to work on busy highways during rush hour, some buses, called "expresses," stop only at a a few places. The buses also have special devices to change traffic lights in their favor.

For travel across the city and surrounding urban areas of California, the L.A. County Metropolitan Transportation Authority (MTA) operates a **subway** line and several **light-rail** lines.

▶ The complex freeway system is the most popular way for people to get around Los Angeles. The roads are built like bridges one on top of the other to provide exits and entrances on to different streets and highways.

Local Government

The **local** government runs the city by making laws and deciding how to spend and raise money. The government leader, the mayor, is assisted by a team of **elected** people.

The city of L.A. has thousands of employees, or workers. They work in different departments to keep residents safe and healthy. An Emergency Preparedness Department helps people during emergencies such as earthquakes.

▼ Just like U.S. citizens elected President Barack Obama to lead the national government, every four years L.A. city residents elect a new mayor to lead the local government.

These firefighters are trying to control a fire in the forests around L.A. Hot, dry weather can start a forest fire. The city's fire department has more than 100 neighborhood fire stations.

About 3,500 firefighters in the Los Angeles Fire Department put out fires and provide emergency medical services. More than 10,000 officers work in the Los Angeles Police Department to solve and prevent crimes, help in emergencies, and direct traffic. The Department of Sanitation helps keep the city clean by picking up and removing garbage and **recyclable** material from households and businesses.

Los Angeles is warm and dry for most of the year. It has a cooler wet season lasting from November to April. In the dry season, the city **conserves**, or looks after, its water by not allowing people to use lawn sprinklers on certain days of the week. In fall, the warm, dry Santa Ana winds blow across the city, sometimes starting forest fires.

This parade in Chinatown, L.A., celebrates Chinese New Year. Other cultures, including Japanese and Thai, also hold new year's celebrations in the city but on different dates.

Events held on L.A. streets, such as the Golden Dragon Parade, Martin Luther King Jr. Kingdom Day parade, Cesar E. Chavez Day march, and Mardi Gras parade, are popular through the year.

The city hosts film festivals and celebrations of cultural heritages. Big events in the city include the Academy Awards, the Los Angeles Marathon, and the Los Angeles Dodgers major league baseball games.

▶ The Day of the Dead Festival, or Dia de los Muertos, includes ceremonial Aztec dances. The day, which has Mexican or Latino origins, honors those who have died.

Los Angeles no longer has any surrounding farmland on which to build more suburbs. To create more homes, big, empty office buildings are being turned into living spaces. Historic buildings are being reworked to help them withstand earthquakes. By holding events in downtown, the center of the city is being better used. This allows the suburbs to remain quiet.

▼ Many L. A. shoppers now use free reusable grocery bags rather than the plastic ones that are thrown away and end up in landfills.

26

A garden started at the Helen Bernstein High School in Hollywood will give students, who live in an urban environment, a chance to get hands-on experience with nature.

To improve city air, L.A. often allows **hybrid vehicles** to park at parking meters for free. This encourages more people to drive these cleaner cars. New green spaces are being created, such as the Los Angeles State Historic Park in downtown that has turned an old railroad yard into areas for picnics, biking, or walking. These plans should make L.A. a better city to live in.

Suburbs Around the World

Suburbs are found in cities all over the world, from Tokyo in Japan, Mumbai in India, to Cairo in Egypt. Some suburbs like those in London, England, are former towns that grew together as they got bigger. In other places, like L.A. and Toronto, Canada, suburbs have their own local governments and make neighborhood laws.

▼ Not all suburbs are built on flat land. This suburb of Sydney, Australia, is made of houses on a hill that overlook the bay.

North American suburbs are often areas with more modern houses and schools compared to those in the inner city. In other parts of the world, suburbs are where new immigrants settle, or where people with low **incomes** live. In these suburbs, often called slums, houses are often poorly made and people face poor living conditions.

Facts and Figures

How many?
Los Angeles contains about 6,500 miles (10,460 km) of streets and 180 miles (290 km) of freeways. There are 2,500,000 vehicles in the city, and 1,980,000 of those are cars.

What's in a name?
The city gets its name from a 1781 settlement named El Pueblo de la Reina de los Angeles. This settlement slowly became a city and its name was shortened to Los Angeles.

By air and sea
Los Angeles has four airports, as well as one of the busiest seaports in the world. Ships come to Los Angeles from all over the world to pick up and deliver all kinds of cargo.

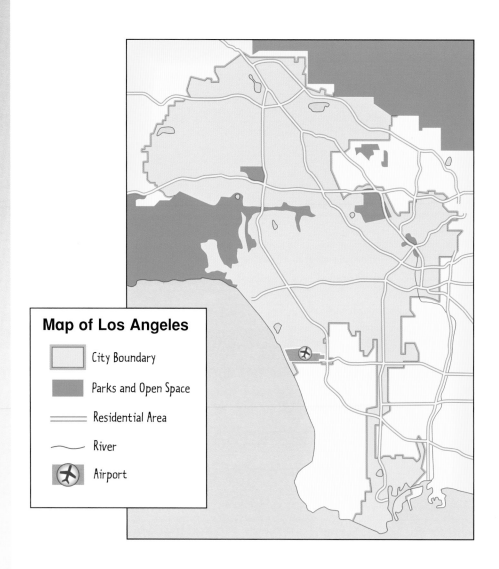

Map of Los Angeles

City Boundary

Parks and Open Space

Residential Area

River

Airport

Glossary

charter school A school run by parents, teachers, and members of a neighborhood

city A large urban area, with thousands or millions of people and many buildings and roads

commerce/commercial To do with buying and selling of goods and services

conserve To save or not waste something

elected Chosen by voting

energy The power to do work. It can come from burning fuels such as coal or oil, or from wind, water, and the Sun

exhaust Gases given off by engines and factories

factories Places where machines are used to make things so they can then be sold. Factories are also called plants

government People who make laws and run a city or country

hybrid vehicles Cars that run on two forms of power, usually gas and electricity

immigrants People moving into an area

income Money earned through work

industrial To do with factories

law A rule that must be obeyed by everyone

light rail A city train meant to be fast and to carry people, not frieght

local People or places that are nearby

neighborhood An area where people live, work, and relax together

population The number of people living in a city

private school A school started and operated privately, without relying on government money

public transportation A system for everyone to use to move around

recyclable Material that can be reworked so that it can be used again

residential To do with houses and homes

residents People who live in a place

resources Things one needs or must have

rural areas Small places to live in the countryside

sewage Wastewater from kitchens and restrooms

suburbs Areas near the edge of a city

subway A city train that travels an underground railroad and tunnels

transportation Moving things from one place to another, or a system that does this

urban areas Built-up places such as a city or big town

Further Information

FURTHER READING

Book of Cities, Piero Ventura, Universe Publishing, 2009.
City Hall: The Heart of Los Angeles, Debbie Bertram, Susan Bloom, and Aileen Leijten, Talifellow Press, 2003.
City I Love, Lee Bennett and Marcellus Hall, Abrams Books for Young Readers, 2009.
City Lullaby, Marilyn Singer, Clarion Books, 2007.
City Signs, Zoran Milich, Kids Can Press, 2005.
What is a Community: From A to Z, Bobbie Kalman, Crabtree Publishers, 2000.
Wow! City! Robert Neubecker, Hyperion Children's Books, 2004.

WEB SITES

Los Angeles Official Website: http://www.lacity.org
Los Angeles for kids: http://kids.lacity.org
Los Angeles Visitors' Bureau: http://www.discoverlosangeles.com
Los Angeles County Almanac: http://www.laalmanac.com/default.htm

Index